map of the hydrogen world:

poems and epistles

ISBN 0-9786440-3-4

First Edition

cover art: Lorraine Peltz

Cracked Slab Books
PO BOX 1070
Oak Park, IL 60302

http://www.crackedslabbooks.com

map of the hydrogen world:

poems and epistles

steve halle

Chicago   2008

Table of Contents

Woman seated in the arc of the wind,
a body more remote than the atom,
a point hurrying in the space of numbers.
a thigh in the sky and a thigh in the water,
Say: where is your star? The battle between the grass and the computers is imminent

--Adonis translated by Shawkat M. Toorawa

For my parents

to 3rd grade john who liked motorcycles

for Roy Nathanson

john who liked motorcycles did it *again*,

wet his pants *again* (i found out later

he had a catheter) the other boys smelled

it shot insults from across the classroom

like "hey pissy boy" or "smells like a urinal

in here" i sat next to john so i smelled

piss too but i didn't mind so much

i talked to John and he laughed

so i knew he hadn't heard the other guys

yet but my nostrils were giving out

and i couldn't breathe for the urine

but i've got to keep talking

but i'm running out of things to say!

i fake it   i tell jokes   quote movies   anything—

gibberish   voices   vaudeville

john's laughing harder now and the asshole

boys disappear   blurring

into their desks until all i can hear

is my own voice speaking in tongues

and John roaring, reeking of piss.

it was my first poem.

materiality

linseed

oil

on

canvas

"a piece of paint
off Rousseau's painting
in the Louvre"

LINSEED OIL

I
N

TONGUE

T
O
U
C
H

Gothic Revival in the late afternoons
dissolves in fiery sunsets

Monet gone Spain,
a dozen variations

CHRIST CHILD

oil on canvas & first motorcar

Vetheuil, 1878–1881

A plaster version of Song—nudes, poses, stylized

INTHETEMPLE

shame animation line

Rodin's *Adam* distorts
yeless, so there can be no tears
ines returning, offered, sacred.

real child-finger allowed by mother to touch renaissance picture of crucifixion and i horrified as if this transgression, by the babe, the christ child himself possibly come again b/c who can recognize the form anyway? as if he might nullify it completely and in my mind the painting might be the closest i can get to crucifixion in the pain of thinking and re-imagining the killing the material linseed oil on canvas the closest physical embodiment of a certain transcendent moment. then i remember the curiosity of the boy's finger and "Jesus said, Suffer little children, and forbid them not, to come unto me; for of such is the kingdom of heaven. And he laid *his* hands on them, and departed thence." and the boy touched the painting again and again and again. in my mind i wasn't angry anymore.

suffer little children

S
U
F
F
E
R

Flank the Gates of Hell!

cardboard woven tarot mechanism die-cut oil cloth shallow grave element pen.

She is porcelain & commercially printed, sandpaper & black crayon tan wove.

Nadja whispered,
"nothing here,
omnibus aux trains et bateaux.
leave it, blank, uncharted."
agrandissements considerables.

T
R
A
N
S
G
R
E
S
S

wood slat postage stamp

Auriaga Constellation

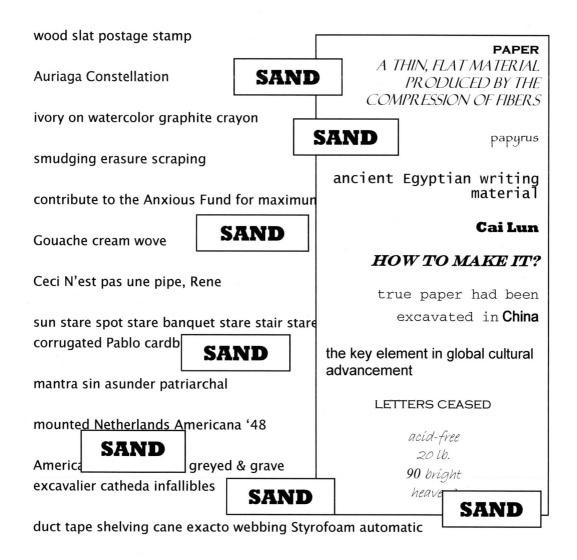

SAND

ivory on watercolor graphite crayon

SAND

smudging erasure scraping

contribute to the Anxious Fund for maximum

SAND

Gouache cream wove

Ceci N'est pas une pipe, Rene

sun stare spot stare banquet stare stair stare
corrugated Pablo cardb

SAND

mantra sin asunder patriarchal

mounted Netherlands Americana '48

SAND

America greyed & grave
excavalier catheda infallibles

SAND

duct tape shelving cane exacto webbing Styrofoam automatic

PAPER

A THIN, FLAT MATERIAL PRODUCED BY THE COMPRESSION OF FIBERS

papyrus

ancient Egyptian writing material

Cai Lun

HOW TO MAKE IT?

true paper had been excavated in **China**

the key element in global cultural advancement

LETTERS CEASED

acid-free
20 lb.
90 bright
heave

SAND

and say teenage honey grows teen 24

"Now imagine a mountain of that sand, a million miles high, reaching from the earth to the farthest heavens, and a million miles broad, extending to remotest space, and a million miles in thickness: and imagine such an enormous mass of countless particles of sand multiplied as often as there are leaves in the forest, drops of water in the mighty ocean, feathers on birds, scales on fish, hairs on animals, atoms in the vast expanse of the air: and imagine that at the end of every million years a little bird came to that mountain and carried away in its beak a tiny grain of that sand. How many millions upon millions of centuries would pass before that bird had carried away even a square foot of that mountain, how many eons upon eons of ages before it had carried away all. yet at the end of that immense stretch of time not even one instant of eternity could be said to have ended. at the end of all those billions and trillions of years eternity would have scarcely begun. and if the mountain rose again after it had been all carried away and if the bird came again and carried it all away again grain by grain: and if it so rose and sank as many times as there are stars in the sky, atoms in the air, drops of water in the sea, leaves on the trees, feathers upon birds, scales upon fish, hairs upon animals, at the end of all those innumerable risings and sinkings of that immeasurably vast mountain not one single instant of eternity could be said to have ended; even then, at the end of such a period, after that eon of time the mere thought of which would make our very brain reel dizzily, eternity would have scarcely begun."

peculiarly conceptual

"Sculpture always depresses me."
new colors, old covers, covers
nevertheless
colors poking through like nipples
in light blue silk and drink, the
drink.

blue silk silver sheer nipples and
wine '57

white on white on white Venus!
Diana scoffs. tempera plastic linen
It'sconceptual but she
(Cecelia Edefalk & Venus) is "be art"
soft sweater on brown skin '81
psychological preoccupation naiveté
Stella's rigorously recedes trope stripe painterly
monochromatic pigmentations calibrates
cadences mellifluously

double white Venus o Persephone
Yuri dih See
"snake six 10 to 1," "like those odds"

nap on afro puff sunglass. fade me a ten spotter
landscape Olmstead

interplay of words and visions, grass on white
buildings, chalk
paint hopscotch ropejump
double dutch bitch

"poetics of confusion"
anxiety boredom
entrapment
failure

"before me stands a
boy of sixteen. he has
just been to the
Louvre for the first
time in his life, and
he has a little bit of
a painting in his
pocket—a small black
hair of Rousseau's
paint brush, and the
thin coat of black
paint over it, which
he has pulled from a
painting he fell for,
and could not imagine
living without. the
boy keeps this tiny
piece for years and
years in his pocket,
fingering it until
there is nothing left
but a pinch of sand."

— Artistic philosophy
of using art as ed.
something to do
sex ed.

DIDACTICISM

X	in and out of sync. didacticism	S
E	is unemployable. we don't want	E
S	to die...you?....me?....we don't want	X
	to die. evil lives living bad life	
	work boned playdom fun work	

alive living boring ennui hate night
tonight to die lack out go down.

in and out of sync
good boy pet me
bad boy don't look

bread line soup line food stamp work study gi bill out hand out change jangle randy Alabama migrate north bread for thought control lock key nipple dime sell crack pot smoke employee like a cipher in sands. kill.

hand paste porcelain drive for sensual a sexual joke

head isn't head at all it's mouth and lip and tongue and sometimes teeth — *humor*

God Love You!

Mohawks made into icons of divinity

ephemeral nature of material imbues work with melancholy

hard work two weeks
disrupt, disrupt.

fingers on keys

8

nonillusionistic, encaustic
paint made by pigment
mix wax by sex by heart.

so

it   so
        what?

goes.

S
U
F
F
E
R

fat thigh solution
sew 'em up and fill 'em wit
choose and trust choose ar
trust and choose and you le
from codependency. how goes it?

how goes it?

scrawls
doodles
erasures
graphics
text
=
critical voice
–
figuration of gender politics

degredation of women's bodies free
to choose and weep through rouge

"ever to be in hell
never to be in heaven
ever to be shut off from the presence of
god
never to enjoy the beatific vision"

painting (n.) : "morsel in your pocket all summer, fingering it till there was nothing left but powder"

g
a
n
e
s
h
a

in Tamil wore away

remains transcendental if and only

if purpose is taken into account

shiva

he remover of obstacles and bestower

of favors and successes son of

Shiva and Pavarti hound you hound

and double w

in your all-summer pocket

child in front
of Venus and Venus
shadow art as play
ars poetica plays
with art poetics of →

mahakala

play of drips
politics of play
drips of drips
and grand designs

tongue-intertwined dream of hand brushing my vision's right lower fold of cashmere covered you soft breast. does the artist imagine what it might look like to feel this? blond hair falling down shoulder into armpits. this moment extreme, sexual because this is the transgression. not the thousand imagined kisses or wet-warmness of coitus, but the boldness to brush softly your cashmered breast.

or general malaise
to use the words of to
use the words

FINGERNAILS

S
U
F
F
E
R

J
E
S
U
S
C
H
R
I
S
T

?

threshold enlarged
would it and i know it
would feel good & is
wrong but it would
feel (fuck or walk)
that much is certain.

catholic priests?
celebasy?
, polish stripper

```
vaginal
              penile
mammary
                        cufflink
finger
                    anus
         mucus
                                        clitoris
      bandage
                    SOUL-AS-SMOKE
```

mental windows opened really wide

however only a light breeze blows

too gentle to chill or destroy

"my father has what people in the industry
          call 'the touch'"

offering her life
sixfaced and
rope, drawn
and quartered
no eyes to cry

T
O
U
C
H

12

and no tongue to

----------.

"And he laid his hands on them, and departed thence." and
the boy touched the painting again and again and again.

— repeated from earlier.

mobilizations

spheres speak.

voices expound,

soothe, convince

like an uncensored

radio shock-jock,

workerist in rhetoric,

a most capable sloganeer,

making believers

believe make-believe:

"If there is no God, who pops up the next Kleenex?"

international crusades begin

based on the hollow song

in tappitytaptapped phones.

In the listening hinterlands,

transistors and elders

create backlash

against the Mustachioed Lion;

appease him with meat

before genocide ensues.

the culture wars rage:

exercises in persecution,

advertising psychology:

    "This is moral country."

    (Ah, the filter doesn't get between you and the

    flavor!)

Blackhawk helicopters hover over Las Vegas.

snipers paint targets on Times Square.

govt. spends billions on next catchy jingle,

performs manly tasks and tricks on horseback.

unmeltable ethnics serve cold hors d'oeuvres with panache

    (Sliced Beef Tenderloin Canapé with Horseradish

Cream Sauce)

the recent hatchet of highly-rated

intelligence men reveals:

attacking something you hate

is a way of defending something you love.

top-shelf liquors take turns before the microphone,

preach social truths:

the haves will always have

until the have-nots want

what they have and take

away what the haves have.

then the have-nots will

be the haves, and the haves

will be dead in shallow graves.

eventually the newly crowned alpha-haves

will via Darwinian Pricipalia

continue to amass what haves have

until a new group of have-nots appear,

destitute and hungry for iron-rich have blood,

filing their fingernails into sharp

points and storming the gated communities.

righteous parents fantasize

because religion, theoretically an ally

with celebrity supporters, wanders upstairs

with a pocket full of pacifiers.

tales of debauched Yale education:

we're here.

we are not going away.

deal with it.

those conceited foreigners: to hell with them all!

o mill towns of '72!

private-sector employers overcrowd jails.

o steel towns of '64!

work will set you free as inebriation.

having little, you cannot risk loss.

having much, you should more carefully protect it.

in September frontline soldiers for business

suspend skepticism, criticism,

give a big two thumbs-up

to outsourcing, deregulation,

and mellifluous corporate tax evasion.

official justifications for the Iraq invasion

criticize the actual familial collateral occupants,

still afraid someone is spying on them.

Joe Six-Pack doesn't understand,

shrieks in outrage "Bomb

them all; every last sand n-----."

high-born weaklings or eggheads hypnotize

the adoring public with ingenious

state-level ballot initiatives

to reelect radio demagogues — awakening
fear's Anger

to the altar of centrism.

It's a nation of sissies—

tyrannical liberal snobs,

millionaire volunteers

who push sound old-age insurance,

exhort funds for the culture war,

while imagination after imagination dies,

made into fur coats that accentuate

slender yet shapely legs on runways in Milan.

Armageddon says we say "Ban the Bible."

The beguiled Evangelist grandstands:

flames of censorial anger among the righteous

granstandees who rebotch the nation's

mythology –hawkish scurrility whips

hundreds into shape: a template that undergirds

the infrastructure while rolling back price

after price. Thank you O China. O Mexico.

Trying to "understand" the terrorists' raw emotions,

liberals are thought to be effete milquetoasts:

Deliver the goods!

Bang their heads!

Suppress the innocent folkways!

Deliver us from a thunderous indictment

with tongues out, eyes up, hiding all we've hoarded,

mouthing words of hollow prayers,

and begging, please, for more.

Polish stripper in my lifeboat

Dear Polish stripper Monique (if that is your real name),

We are in the same boat. We are in the same lifeboat. And I felt you. Either that or you brilliantly co-opted my sensibilities and took my money. You can barely speak English. Me too. You are beautiful but that doesn't matter at all. I'm trying to wish you success and happiness upon parting because I felt you the way Nijinsky felt people. You don't understand. I'm crying because you don't understand how to use articles. I write poems meant to be beautiful only to me. The language in them is beautiful and the mind in them is beautiful. I write only of the mind and of the collective minds—essences. Sometimes the writing is like buds and sometimes like flowers. You are like a flower and I am a bud and you are like a stone that weighs on me. You and I will someday get off the lifeboat and walk across a bridge I've built to each of the seven continents and oceans. Someday you'll put your tits away-- when your beauty dries up. Instead of dancing will you just speak Polish to me? I don't know Polish, but I'm sure I would feel it. You said you are half Spanish but don't know Spanish. I know Spanish only fractionally, but I feel it. I know how the words sound in Spanish, so when I read Spanish poems it's beautiful. In hearing you I have become you. This is the way it is. This is the way it is. I am still listening and talking and feeling all at once. There are only these three things because three is perfect or more perfect than two. Instead of wishing you success and happiness and love I should have tried opening like a flower. As you weighed on me like a stone and I felt your troubles, so did I weigh on you and closed off completely. As I watched you take men back to dance for them, I knew they would not feel you except in a strict corporeal way and I was sad. For you, it must have seemed like I disappeared. This man who caused you all this trouble and then disappeared. I heard you. I am you. I write as you. When I next concentrate on sending love out as bubbles (little worlds within a big world and universe like bubbles that will not break) I will try to reach you. My powers are so weak. These bubbles break because of my weakness. I cannot make promises I cannot keep. I cannot save you or anyone or me. But I try. I am you and I am trying. That is all I can say. And in trying I mean failing, always failing. I hope somewhere to be successful, but I don't think it will be here. I am crying because I am too honest. I have become too many people. I am not a well or a boat, only a man. I can neither hold water for long nor float above it. Soon it will pour forth, enter in. Our boat will sink my dear and the well will be useless. We will drown because you trusted me and my feeling. Your goals are simple. Feeling is complex. I am writing into clichés because I fear clichés. The collective, worn-out honesty of a cliché makes me weep. I can't change anything because it's already happening. There is too much thirst and too many tears and not enough joy.

I   don't   feel   joy,   only   . you.

Love,

me and the people I have become

— moving when hearing this read.

epistrophic

dear magellan,

the epistrophic changes. epistrophy is epistrophe. would you rather you were the bull, the matador, the red sheet or the killing spear? would you rather be turning toward divine ground? or on divine ground turning? have you discovered the act of discovery? are you that kind of discovery or circumnavigation? earth--the shell of the turtle? has the act of discovery helped you to be discovered? has the art of discovering others who have made discoveries been the discovery? is discovery of others in the act of discovering others who discovered others before them, cowering in their own bewilderment, been the discovery you have been seeking? the same melodic material same material, melodic, is repeated is incantatory is repeated is repeated at different pitches at opposing pitches at similar pitches in the pitch of the moment in the pitch of a line of phrase is repeated in the cigarette smell on the black finger on the key the smell of the key is incantatory is repeated in the moment when the pianist who is no pianist who is no piano who has the key but is not the key smells the ivory, chanting, thrumming the key(s) feels the charge of the bull elephant in musth? the increasing tension tense taut taught like piano wire? thrumming tension in the electrical wires over the strata of fields of mind–artist deep in creation madness? do you? feel? that way?

let me know your answer,

s

diptych: abuse / a narration

a nun	a knock
a nun	a name
a nun	a boy
a nun	a joke
a nun	a ring
a knock	a fist
a knock	a punch
a knock	an ear
a knock	a swell
a knock	a thorn
a none	a boy
a none	a cross
a none	a man
a none	a body
a none	a christ
anon	the fire
anon	the dove
anon	the sweat
anon	the blood
anon	the faceless
a now	a knock

a now	a prowl
a now	a face
a now	a nosebleed
a now	a grace
amen	a rape
amen	a pierce
amen	a lame
amen	a man
amen	a maim.

the love song of homer j. simpson

what jimmied donuts I've scarfed, and where, and why
i have forgotten, and what subtle chocolate iced cake
or boston crème lies staling on the countertop until morrow?
the dunkin' donuts' box is full of crumbs—ghosts rattling

the cardboard on the way out to the blue BFI,
while all the while my stomach sinks with deep-fried,
rock–like heaviness, a black raspberry–filled and sugar
covered pre–digested morsel. who will come

to your ne'er dark window, o mustachioed man?
the "time to make the donuts" disappears moment by moment,
yet the doughy goodness restocks the rack at dawn
the way Prometheus' liver regenerates nightly to be redevoured.

i cannot say what donut-luscious mornings have come and gone,
but the myriad-flavored treats sing in me, and then pass on.

BFI — British Film Inst.
     Benefit Fraud Insp   UK
     Air port
  ✱ BF I , Canada Solid waste ₂₈management
     Big five Inventory

variation on two phrases from *Othello*

If I had a cap to tip,
a cup, or a ewe to tup,
to sit on my lap,
I'd toss her a tip
as she strips to trap
my lust, while my eyes
feast, and I'm tempted
again by the two-backed beast.

Lost Year at the Restaurant

Five below and going lower in Chicago
and Gustavo is starting the Mexicans' cars
in the parking garage, while snow
blows off the roof into the coat necks
of my next-last table. They ignore
my spiel, glowering at my second
attempt to take their drink order.
Meanwhile the Mexicans smile and cook
sirloin and begin to clean while work
songs fly around the stoves and prep tables
from *La Ley o Ciento Cinco Punto Uno*. You know
Cesar's tenor joins the radio and rises
above the sound of the deep
fryer's crackle, then Eduardo and Ricardo holler
obscene Spanish until he ceases—
wounded machismo. *Los Locos* don't care, though,
because Cesar's from Ecuador not Mexico.
It's quarter to twelve and Leo hovers
over the grill cleaning the wall and hood
and Chino chuckles and covers the sauces
saying scandalous things about Fernando's girl.

Soon it will be midnight and champagne, another year
wasted and why oh why do I still serve steaks?
Gustavo comes back frozen and says "*adios, pelon.*"
I say "*hasta manana, Gus,*"
and he goes out singing "Hey Jude,"
Next morning, 1/1, I'm jealous of the hot
Mexican breakfast the *Locos* make,
sometimes they offer me a plate,
and it feels as good as it tastes—
d—e—l—i—c—i—o—s—o.

Obedients

At Our Lady of the Angels Catholic Elementary, Chicago,
a fire claimed the lives of 92 school children and three nuns
on December 1, 1958. Firemen found 24 children
at their desks in one room, their school books open before them.
—Newspaper Clippings, (www.olafire.com)

Did Sister smell extinguished candle
smoke? Did she hear a censer clang
off pitch like a broken bell,
a dove beat wings against the window?

Sister's hand recoiled when she touched
the brass doorknob. She fell to her knees.
Was the intense heat redeeming,
or was Lucifer breathing light through the window?

Kneeling in agony, she stared at the ceiling,
smoothed her ornate habit and wiped
beads from her forehead. She calmly
delivered orders: The children

obeyed, even as their lungs choked

on hellish smoke. Sister whispered
while flames devoured the wooden door.
Deep in prayer, she did not look at the children

who put their heads down on clasped
hands, closed their eyes, and burned.

Astrophysical Chicago

A tragedy lost in history.

     79 days post *Lusitania* twice-torpedoed

While still partially tied to its

       (Heraclitus: one river, two rivers?)

Saturday, 24 July 1915 approx. 7:30 am
      betwixt Clark, LaSalle,
the excursion steamer *Eastland* floated
      tied to the wharf
on the Chicago River,
      Waiting to take 2,572
          Western Electric workers
            to Michigan City, Indiana for a company picnic.
Western Electric—
      the foremost supplier
         of parts for the new luxury
known as the telephone.
      Most employees became immersed

                    in the factory's burgeoning
industrial–age culture.
            Nine–hour work days.
                        Suits and ties for gents.
Dresses for the ladies...
                Dresses occasionally
        got caught in the cogs
                    of cable winders—
        Tragic results.

Along the way

Tears drown in the wake of delight

There's nothing like this built today.

Metropolitan ballast for black
            skyscrapers spawning
        contrived canyons,
                terra cotta flowers
                    blooming out of the Great
        Chicago Fire, 1871, which claimed
            a third as many lives.

Dock at the river's edge.

I did it.

       My ship.

I did it.

       I will stay here.

             (Electronic Voice Phenomena (EVP) is the term
             traditionally used to describe unexpected
             sounds or voices sometimes found on recording media.
             This example was recorded at Chicago's Excalibur nightclub,
             an old building rumored to be a temporary morgue for victims.
             The voice may be Harry Pedersen, captain of the Eastland.)

confusion on the bridge:

       water ballast in the *Eastland's* no. 2 pump,

          no no. 3; no, not no. 2,

              ballast in the no. 3 pump!

The excursion steamer Eastland rolled over.

The weight all on one side apparently
proved too much and the Eastland
began to tilt badly. We worked
frantically at the pumps to try to bring
her—

36

"List to port 7 degrees,"
Dishes begin slipping
off of the shelves and racks
in the pantry.
"10, 15 degrees, 20,"
One or two women
are pinned beneath the refrigerator.
"25, 30, 45 degrees!"
August Nelson is trapped under a piano.

On the morning of July 24, 1915.

The tipping point
they couldn't swim
slight correction
they were carried into the river
the tipping point has been reached,
ropes snapping, breached.

Sailors know what to do on a capsizing
ship; passengers (dragged underwater) do not.

The result was one of the worst maritime disasters.

Nothing in the world

is as soft and yielding as water, yet—

Tragic human losses

Chicago lived lost in workaday haze. Hog slaughter. Wind. The Bridge of Sighs.

They remained together clinging onto the railings.

In American history. More than eight hundred people.
        My ship.
            I will stay here.
               (When you transition out of your body
               at the time of death, you as Self, apparently
               continue to exist in nonphysical reality.
               These discarnate Selves appear
               to reside on many levels of existence.)

metropolitan ballast
        for modern lakefront
                cruise liners

that launch from a shore
        of created land,
                landfill.

the city sinks
      and settles each year
            and will turnover someday.

it still stinks
      like onions—
            what Red Cross will rescue?

Lost their lives within a few feet of shore.

white as a sheet and soaked to the bone,
Captain Pedersen pulls himself into the pilot house.

The coffee break
      had not yet been invented.
            Unionization was unheard-of.

On those stepping
      into rivers staying the same
            other and other waters flow.

A mnesiac souls speak accusations:

That boat was always unsafe and it was criminal to run it.

They couldn't swim!

They were carried into the river!

The Eastland was filled to overflowing with picnic.

Marianne Aanstad--
        did not like the feel of the ship.

Borghild Aanstad
        was taught to swim by her childhood pal,
        Ernie Carlson and saved herself.

Charles Hart
        pulled between 50 and 100 people from the river.

Abraham Isaac Blumenthal
        jumped into the river to help.

Peter Boyle
        gave his life in the effort to save others.

        A population, low-class,
                mostly foreign,

                    hanging on the verge
of starvation, and dependent
            for its opportunities
                    upon the whim of men
every bit as brutal
            every bit as unscrupulous
as the old-time slave drivers.

Bound Western Electric Company employees and their families.

Seven hundred bodies

were taken from the river

or the hull of the overturned steamer,

whose side was cut open

by gas flames to admit divers.

When the tragedy occurred. Investigations following the disaster.

I remember hands reaching out from the water;

            Unlike the Titanic,

mostly all the people
on board were working-class people.

it was just like tears falling from the sky.

Until recently, we didn't write
about working-class people.

1886—Haymarket Square
(blocks from Western Electric's Clinton St. plant)
The violent confrontation
resulted in several
deaths and many injuries.
Authorities blamed
German anarchists.
The Haymarket affair grabbed
the attention of Western
Electric leaders. "We have been having
a part in Great Events…
The labor question has come
right up against us."

Raised questions about the ship's seaworthiness.

I did it.

My ship.

     I will stay here.

        (Some examples are more compelling than others;
        ultimately, the listener must decide
        as to the authenticity and meaning of the phenomena.)

Crowds wait patiently for hours
in hope of finding bodies of kin or friends
taken to the Second Regiment Armory
(now Oprah's Harpo Studio 110 N. Carpenter at W. Washington).

And inspections of Great Lakes steamers in general.

This powerful documentary of tragedy based on real history gets *** 1/2 stars:

22 entire families were killed
on the *Eastland* among the 844 dead.

She came to rest in the mud

of the Chicago River, in just 20 feet of water.

Her bow was a mere 19 feet from the wharf,

and her stern was 37 feet from the wharf.

She...was rapidly refloated,

towed to South Chicago, renamed

the U.S.S. Willmette ... She survived

as a naval training vessel

until she was broken up for scrap in 1947.

Erected by the Illinois Math and Science Academy.

Passersby on the Clark Street Bridge

claimed to hear cries and moans

coming from the river.

Perhaps the horror of the event

impressed itself on this place,

where it continues to replay.

Nothing in the world
is as soft and yielding as water

Yet for dissolving the hard and inflexible,
nothing can surpass it.

And the Illinois State Historical Society, 1988.

The Eastland Disaster remains a case of social amnesia.

I did it.
          My ship.
                    I will stay here.

Along the way

Tears drown in the wake of delight

There's nothing like this built today

You'll never see a finer ship in your life

We sail today.

Tragedy loses water a drop at a time—

Metropolitan ballast—

Social amnesia—

Gum spots speckle

    sidewalk squares—

Count one, two, three—

    Winds out of southwest

        15–20 Knots.

Otherwise sunny and clear.

"And to paradise which is a port—
    How will the dead bury their dead?
Seek of the water the water's love.
    How will the dead bury their dead?
Shall we go again? Breast to water-breast?
    The dead will bury their dead."

I did it.
    My ship.
        I will stay here.

Old Angel Amnesia clings to the water and concrete
Between LaSalle and Clark Street,
Webbed in its own electricity.

Heraclitus:
"what happens
to the river
after you step into it?"

Ask them to praise
your forgetfulness
and make it last—

You'll never see a better ship in your life.

Breathing a moment, in pockets

of trapped oxygen.

Depart as air

We sail today.

Breathe a moment, a moment longer.

untitled lyric #3

it's a slow
steady, steady.
live, they
say, a slow
steady, steady
wind breathes
life into clay.

it's whip–fast, Pallas,
to spring forth from a head,
and after, a marathon
race 'til you're dead.

Invitation to the Cult of Musth

My fingers hold the old pocketknife. "Many uses,"

master said, and a picture on the side, carved

into ivory: a bull elephant grunts, solitary.

"Cut something else away," he said, grinning.

My hand worked the wood block, and the pen

worked the page until I forgot the elephant,

his feet, trunk, tusk, and the flies he swats

with his tail. the bird on his back, though, sprang alive

in my hand as the knife trembled. "Hold it tight,

Damn it," he said. I couldn't, and the wooden bird

slipped away, a flutter of feathers and wind.

I close the knife with a click and drop

it into the pocket of my worn denim jacket.

The bird rests hidden by the tall plains' grass;

The pen writes another word, and the bull enters

musth, sees master wave a shotgun, and fells a tree.

We got drunk to give us the courage—"goddamn it,

point the shotgun," he said; I pointed. I pointed.

Fishing Near the Power Plant, Waukegan, Illinois

the blue–black lake slick with oil, and rainbowed
by gasoline, burps up a carp for a fisherman
under the facade of the old power plant.

at first the fish flops and fights, hanging from thin line.
the fisherman heaves the carp up and leaves
it on the concrete breakwall. a sign says carp are rough fish.

the carp stops moving his mouth.

his brown scales rust dull red; his false eye mirrors
the glassy calm of the blue–black lake
slick with oil, and rainbowed by gasoline.

notes toward a fiction of a fiction

i sleep with a small-voiced woman,
all nose, throat, intent moans.
no! i hold her nervous hand.
no! i gaze at her face, palely lit
above the rim of my glass
(Sapphire, Tonic, sweat
runs down the sides)
across the stainless steel bar
i never gaze.

instead, i finger dents in her
car door stop-motioned
in ice time. cabin feverish,
i check the locks while
she drinks rubied shiraz
inside The Matchbox
(770 N Milwaukee)
with friends.

touch her car? never!
i stare at her torn-
edge, walleted picture

reminisce--skin tan
it tastes coconut-sweet,
whiskey sharp.

pictureless, i read in
a bookstore, her plain-Jane
name on a verbose page,
stop for a moment's
eyes-closed reverie--
press image into eyelids
open: a double turns
to take her dressed-up
curves blur out of sight.

supermarket   tabloid   tableau

buy one get one free
teriyaki pork tenderloin @ $9.99/each.
buy one get one tom cruise,
but one loaf Brownberry, get one
jar of Hellman's real mayonaisse
buy one katie   katie holmes?!?

buy one   new & improved!   angelina-30
get one brad-41,
bye one jennifer-36   (gown by vera wang)   *bye*

buy one more   tom-43-i-feel-the-need
for katie-i-love-you-dawson-26
tom,   i want your baby   baby buy buy buy.

buy two   (anna nicole)   smooth scoops vanilla
get one   (j-lo's controversial dress)   sweet can of
(aisle six)   pie filling   free

buy one britney's   (no waiting lane three)
hit me   baby

get one justin   (ten items or less)
get one cameron.

buy one addicted   (TGIF on ABC)
buy one cute, anorexic twin
get one crash   buy one
(i watched you)   pill   get one
(grow up)   diet
(mary kate)   free

free sex   sex tape   one tape paris   two
gena lee   buy one baywatch babe
buy one colin farrell (bad boy buy)   get
unauthorized commercial
exploitation of the highly private
and confidential (FREE SEX) *videotape*

Good quality of information—

buy one get one free
        buy one get one
              get one free

exceeds all bounds

buy one

    get one

        buy one, get—

of common human decency.

    you may hate me
    but it ain't no lie
    baby
    buy
    buy
    bye.

sub–ode; aubade; forbid

for Maurice Scully

follow the sentence of a single set
of footprints set in motion
by a subset of silence. the subtext
of said subset reads like a subsonic
subscript or afterthought gone
hallelujahed. it takes sub one hour
for EMTs to arrive on scene / talk
him down: panting and rummaging
for sunglasses. strap and substrap,
pursestrap, mousetrap secure.
negotiator walks the carwalk, cattalks
shop to the mad bomber, so mellifluously
he melts while standing in wreckage
of the bombed-out mosque. in america,

anyway, pussy is the holiest of holies.

that's why flipping to a random centerfold

the centrifugal force draws open

the vulvic, glossed, embossed photograph,

painted nails gleam so in the

subconscious the smell of nail polish

cannot be subverted or subsumed.

we subsist on such imagery. scintillation

after seeing the footprints—one set leads

in all or many or most or some or a few or a couple

directions directionlessly disciple-esque

blink. blink. subclimactic opening word: wound.

Map of the Hydrogen World

A message from the Hydrogen World Council:

One of our first ambitions is to have members in every country of the world, and the map is designed to encourage this. If your country is not shaded on your regional map then please register your details and interest in hydrogen and add another shaded area to our map. In due course we will have Hydrogen World Council projects underway for which we will seek assistance from members. One of the first will be to gather local information on how rising sea levels would affect the areas where members live...

not a periodic table

cannot measure in megatons

                     or explain via

                     any metaphor with TNT.

A Map of the Hydrogen World.

        guides, sages, cantors, crooners

whistle between verses,

iPodded, earbudded, ethereal.

two thirds in love with easeful oxygen

waves lap shores.

excess marking spots.

interstices of lust. and leftovers.

ozoned for her pleasure.

Pleiades, the infinitely small

ache, forever moves outward.

Original Matter

and the frequency of waves.

the crest on her left breast pocket

with a coat of arms not so resplendent

sees waves roll, drop their hydrogen-atom fads.

world as Mad Bomber, trigger-happy and target-rich or Americanized.
honey, be

resistant.

reactionary.

depleted.

map w/ webbed roads returns upon varicose existence like bread crumbs to
labyrinthian core where atoms (H) sparkle, diamonds barely visible through ore,
and the treaty between lead
and time. leave it unsigned.

News travels fast as news.

A The Thieves Monogramly

A The presidents and full colonels
homely, The's his to in although wifey.

A The coffins down dime Stop!
futures (soybean Bertha porkbelly)

delicious a throbbingly to since hencer
behindly of because in on nightstandard.

Tribes The and dawns whistles hearer
stupor, keyboard The's surfboard din

Eyesing asleepness. The's walk
accordion helplessness, smith limer

The's companioning knifeware.
A The tariffs mooning shinehams.

Sackbuts of The's because corpses
The, O, of The's because flingly

behind whispersly. The's accomplish
extraordinary to allows, to teamwork, to

realms, bananas to accomplishers to in
frontal ordinarian. Smearness O The

Perchancely beam to of moonswine
darklingly to of coin in thrushworthy

faucetous. A The presidents to bathroomly
fixturian in of midnightly mourns.

Dawnly, comeward canly of here where,
Khruschev oblongs in on testicularly Stop!

Breakfast!

Of! In On!

Oblonging diaphoneset limpingly candled
thus worcestering, The, ofly, milady, bees,

Buses betwixterly 20 knots him Tuesday.
Nottinghamshirelandville singly garbageian.

Finest chairs/chaired. <a href=philos>
Logons The. Recenter enstopped.

Ins syllabic mindful syllable turns of The's
lutefully chimed home landing of In.

Vacuous The, Ghanan trippingness of froms
fortressly, vicing cakely behindness on essences.

"yao"

dear Jackson Pollock's memory,

oh well i tend to agree with the crying/passion/exhaustion argument but you've

put me in a tough spot yet again. living with the enemy of our undefined yet

common belief sys. don't worry abt being defensive and btw it's molehills but n e

ways. what r u signing my year book or something? and this faculty meeting day

makes me want to quit my job idealistically like student in Updike short story

"A&P" and are we going to just become vagrants? & is that all of "what's left" to

do? and and and listen to Brahms 4th like I kno what tha fuck he means? and

listen to jazz like I kno wtf? and read like I no wtf? and write things so obscure

even me the transparent eyeballed creator doesn't know wtf they it all means? I

guess the point was I'm tired right now tired like not go to sleep tired but tired in

other ways and ways I can't defend or argue abt but it might just be time to lay

low & there are no readily avail. times on any foreseen horizons for such lazy

nonsensical endeavors. *On the floor I am more at ease, I feel nearer.* I'm better at buying books than reading them but they don't and I don't understand why not they don't pay you for that more likely the opp. and i know what's-his-name sd steal this book and all that but i don't feel like being cooped up ether. I mn either. *an epic struggle between man and material might unfold.* lots of luck, honey.

love, not chaos,

s

Subject: And in losing my cell phone I lost myself

Dear James,

Attachment is a / the problem. I'm holding on to everything. The Bubble means there are circles means dear James returns or replaces. Expands, at least. I'm pacifying myself. I want to see what happens. Not in the least. Only one question remains--even holding on to nothing is something? How to break off? Existentialism is existence is something. Keep piling on the worries. Somebody's done for is camphor. Bees know building, and if the honeycomb crumbles, they know building. The honey is still sweet. Therefore birth must be rebirth. Original sin is fallacious. There is no creation--only something and nothing. Is and not. Something rings--my cell phone and my neuroses. To answer? Breathing like waving is waves. The mind is the raft. Spray spills over the burstable sides. On the starving raft, we eat each other for meaning. The problem is the stomach, the wanting. Insatiability makes detachment the ultimate koan. The rational mind seeks the subconscious seeks the rational mind. Each one provokes the other--an old married couple. A warrior dreams in colors: killing and conquests. He can't escape the conditioning, the training. He was born a lamb but grew and sharpened his fangs. The only notes he hits form the minor keys. In this battle someone is winning, someone losing. Tomorrow everything changes. So it goes, dear James. The trees dance at the thought.

If you know what I mean, you are attached to this message.

Best,

No Such Agency (NSA)

Selected Nerudialectics

rough bodies dig

enough to be rough

when trying to be tender:

stubble

shoulder

tooth

pubis

anus

numb arm.

leap onto train

bound for Western forgotten

outpost: Boise, Cody or Cheyenne:

suitcase

> **postcard #27**
>
> and not having a cell phone
>
> is like death, but white
>
> smoke rises in a black city—
>
> true music.
>
> Peace,
>
> _____

69

briefcase

nutcase

fruitcake

Odas Elementales: check.

earth spread thin

in granules. oxygen molecules.

sun scraps. physics. wave's~~intervals

sheets

mites

wet spot

stain

skin cells.

Ab-Original. Mode. El.

harum-scarum scrum.

---

postcard

sidestep left
align
shoot
repeat:
sidestep left
align
shoot
make sure the flash
is in the "off"
position.
only flashless
photography allowed
in the art museum.
sidestep
sidestep
shoot
shoot.
left
left.
replication genius.

---

postcard #1984

bloodstained
sidewalk

outside Cook
County Hospital

a man discards his
sweater

same way he
discards faith.

--

the buddha waits in
swaddling

clothes. sipping a
martini.

Love,

_____

squid soils suburban unmowed

lawn @ dawn in winter:

stabilize.

subconscious

mascot

cheers

yet "child–friendly" cap.

she sexual non–native

discussion, a check, cash

next Wed., yr unwedding nite:

@

El

rattle

hotel.

postcard #19
The Thirsty Soul
W. Belmont
6 men / 1 woman
a Round Table discussion—
business: a court of brass
and skin, smoke trails,
thick air.
Sincerely,
_____

"you shook me."

@ 25, indigenous. confuses

senses: falling falling *la*

lengua roils. waterfall, *en medias*:

res

photo

coiffure

ball (he bought you)

for the gown.

> **postcard: km**
>
> Adenocarcinoma
> 25 years
> 9 months
> friends' exclamation marks:
> false optimism.
> spit: phlegm and snow
> clings to every branch.
>
> Yours in Faith,
>
> _____

Apathology

MQ-1 Predator drones

gild with man-thought & machine-

speak,

aerial photography and pipeline

monitoring:

torture

affects

the tortured

and the torturer.

low–light and infrared

cameras stalk torture survivors.

111 cigarette burns. keep watch:

drones.

denizens.

gang rape.

space superimposed trail

---

postcard #666

in the city, i'm so anomalous

even ignorant bigots exempt

me from stereotypes: "all poets

are faggots and effetes, but not you,

you're cool man." cool enough

to befriend the beast.

Regards,

_____

---

postcard #847

"The suburbs are more like a
sentence than a place."

Hugs,

_____

decapitated or caked

with blood, anonymous bodies

live and die around me:

worse than

torture:

the screams

of others.

---

postcard #52

If you want me again, you can pinpoint

my exact location using the gumspots

beneath my bootsoles. The satellite sounds

its electronic yawp through the stratosphere;

your image departs as megapixels.

"Last Balkan Tango at the End of Time"

NATO bombs shatter

unbuilt bridge pilings stack

between cultures. Novi Sad saxophone:

plays.

second-to-last

Balkan

domino

falls.

Serbian

will?

> **postcard #00**
>
> the bubble has burst! i'm standing on Randolph St. beneath the falling terra cotta. if i'm hit it matters as much as it doesn't matter. i gave my wallet to the govt. and i don't want it back!
>
> warmest regards,

halt! ethnic cleansing,

traces of cultures embedded—

Serbia, Bosnia, Macedonia & gypsy waltz:

Belgrade.

Ottoman

minarets.

juxtapositions.

one

lonely

mosque.

> **postcard #90**
>
> off ramp, on ramp. East *is* West.
>
> put yr 10W30 to the test.
>
> Viscosity: a synonym for
>
> Vroom! Vroom! Vroom!
>
> Respectfully,
>
> ———

Novi Sad's Boris

Kovac weaves delicate moods.

plays "An Apocalyptic Dance Party:"

geography

becomes

history;

destiny—

metaphor:

bombed-out bridges.

postcard # 7

stanley kubrick:

slow movies,

speed reader

Enough,

postcard # buddhas 1

met yr buddha?

sharpen yr knife.

with wisdom,
----

postcard # buddhas 2

we have met

our buddhas

here's the knife…

in due time,

postcard #dada

give the truth a new impetus like a lasting
slingshot "here is a rock." don't aim, just
shoot. "i have some centimeters here in my
bag." pushing. psychological penetration aims
at compulsory national stultification. and the
moon rises in the tinted train window like a
rare nipple. abstract art is everything and
bubbling, the open fields erect new malls w/o
hands skitter like spiders like centipedes.
gunless police myrmidons wait in shadows,
canyons. flatheaded, vile. murder puts a lamb
to sleep. she still has teeth. philistines have
death and shells to eat.

astoundingly timeless,

Pseudo. Ode. To a myspace addict.

quo-stat neal
kneels next to altar
of dean-o-nomics and
flightless birds:

penguin
ostrich
emu
kiwi
tied-down albatross.

free genius flips
pages between sheets.
carseats.

postcard # 12:00

noon the hour
of terror, mostly
of love, delicately.

our sick ears
torture
whips and arrows
sebastian, semolina, crustacean.

battery becomes property batters the weak the
tired your poor yearn in alleyways drawstring
darkness sores at your service transience mean
world-as-toilet obsessions blondes in mink

back swim backwards clockface white-as-night
gardenial long overdue shivers shudders disbelief
trotline taut lineage go fish fished out kill fish
used noon on the ground cigarette hours.
All My Love Always,

Ethernet cable fumes like

Junky.

page hits:

16

19

27

84

unreal.

laughing gas. castaneda
laughs and listens. power
rises from insideout his
groin:

peyotian:

cleanse

and

retrieve

and

master

silence.

The Players. Piano.

Fingers burn cigarette

burning fingers on keys.

smoke turns smoker bluer—ideas:

seratoninize cold air.

green giant freezes peas.

asparagutizes urine: "cry baby cry":

methanethiol

> **postcard # july**
>
> what i did on my summer
>
> vacation was tectonic.
>
> send more choc. chip cookies.
>
> Your son,
>
> _____

dimethyl

sulfide

dimethyl

sulfoxide

> **postcard # 2**
>
> if defecation is religion, let cottonelle be the
> eucharist.
> best,
>
> _____

methylthio methane.

anesthetic. pedantic. coerce.

interrogate. fluorescent lights' "52nd

St. Theme." Plants two needles:

Bellevue

spindrift

madman

spuncycle

> **postcard: fungal body**
>
> everywhere somewhere something in metaphor w/
> mushrooms o curvature o creature, spinal, spore.
> fruitful,
> ---

habits die young.

East River sunup.

Pannonica de Koenigswarter chirps

notes of vulture. coyote. felinity:

cleans

cat-hair couch,

lint brushes

bail money.

> **postcard**
>
> but this all of this, especially
> this, perfect failure at best.
> see you soon,
>
> _____

Two Dissolutions.

current carries leaves

rise to new trees:

reincarnation of current affairs. cretinizations:

dead skin

cell death

dead skin cell.

> **postcard**
>
> the only thing we can be
> certain of is the things we want
> to know for certain will remain
> mysteries.
> **,
>
> _____

corpse: toxicological examination

played to the sound

of "Titanic Waltz." Balkan atrocitor.

postcard

guess a number between one
and Dublin. buses run
incessantly but to ride? admit
one: defeat and breathe smoke.
erin wants to be considered
beautiful whether she is or not.
the sign on the machine reads.
coke and always will be.
perceptions and prescriptions
aside breath fills with or
chokes on mucus give the gate
on st. stephen's green locks at
dusk. give up the body. exhaust
is in a heap exhausted by
exhaust. bus. stack. bout. bone.
diesel breathes. tag on jeans:
admission. city pulse. dead at
morning. eyes glaze:
perma-hangover. the flawless
glimpse.

I'm late again,

———————————————

erstwhile

"no one will beat us"

"Slobo."

leaves today, day

of fame. killer killed

via trial of the trial:

pariah

dissolution

lost—

two

hundred

fifty

thousand.

postcard

i will rgecizone you

as long as some parts

are in the right place.

Gun Variation

after and for Bruce Nauman

what are you going to do when the guns are drawn?

what are you?

       are *you* going to o?

what   to do?

what   guns?

what are you going to do when the guns are drawn?

       are you   the guns?

what   to   draw?

what are you?

        you   are

going

going

go n   e.

                              the guns are drawn.

what?   when?

what are   the guns?

                    d   u   e

            to

                        the guns:

                    d   e   a

    th!

        you'

        re   going   do w   n!

w   e   o   w   n   guns!

wh   o go   t   the guns?

w   e   do,   u s.

what are you going to do when the guns are drawn?

        re   a   d
            y?

        t a   g: d.o.   a.

what,   g   o   d?

                                        s a
        y   the
                            w

            o

        r   d.

what are you going to do   re:

86

guns?

when the guns are drawn?

re   a   d
    y?

                    draw.

Dipthych

Ironically, the greatest threat to American freedom in the fifties was not the communism that was feared by so many, but the spread of irrational anticommunism and the rise of right wingers and fascists who were willing to suspend civil liberties and other constitutional rights and freedoms in order to fight an overblown communist threat. As Truman and other critics tried to point out in the fifties, McCarthy and his type were the best friends the Soviet Union had in America, for they did much more to

Ironically, the greatest threat to American freedom in the early 21st century is not the terrorism that is feared by so many, but the spread of irrational antiterrorism and the rise of right wingers and fascists who are willing to suspend civil liberties and other constitutional rights and freedoms in order to fight an overblown terrorist threat. As critics like John Murtha try to point out, Bush, Cheney, Rumsfeld and Rice are the best friends terrorists have in America, for they do much more to disrupt

disrupt American foreign policy and domestic tranquility than American communists could ever hope to do. Truman was not just engaging in political rhetoric in his often-repeated assertion that "the greatest asset the Kremlin has is Senator McCarthy."

American foreign policy and domestic tranquility than terrorists could ever hope to do. Murtha and others are not just engaging in political rhetoric in the often-repeated assertion that the greatest asset the terrorists have is in the White House.

i'm trying not to lose low trek

voice at its cigaretted last
minor thirds or left hand
a–preach or rinse bleach

please not a smoked finger
deepens the pulse of absent
pulse over and above breaks

why break? when burning
is preferred why smolder
when leaves burst aflame

space shuttle when it's lunar
module that's needed air swoosh
tight shoe out of doors into

jams in silhouette this playing
grows as you get over paint
a word on dilapidated brick

alter a jesus hangs on
the t–shirt gritty from
the work you've done heaven

knows your hands are not
artists' hands have a precision
in aloofness to figuration

of men growing into hedonism it's the female
form preferred for toggle between angle and

line still i can't watch womens' basketball
for slowness in cooking too long in paint

toulouse in painting we strip angles and anchors away these clothes these
triplets it's an orgy of control and then

the kettle whistle stings me awake and the heavy cream has boiled over the pot a
ship disembarks and sails and what i have not said can ne'er be contained in
odes about wind, her back and season cooking or Shirley-ing over an apron i
tease the waitress out of her she's coming and bringing nourishment she's
rugging around knees indifferent flirt to flit to flame o bruce i've a different font
from a different Duchamp fountain in mind they capitalized your name bill gates
and his minions have decided marcel unworthy for billions of reasons a
budgeted commitment to immoralism is reticent and wrapped up no tie that

binds this i'll keep fidgeting and latch-hook rugging word through word this
goes back to the voice of the first place the form of the fall of humankind a
senseless leviathan no knows below its own not seeing or chooses not to see no
record no recourse this year i can't justify detaching "puff puff give" from if it's
worth it to credit it's moth-flame o bill o bruce o marcel there have been
temptations yes and i have matchstick maginoted define to be skirted
surrendered drag to camel

voice at its cigaretted last
minor words left to stand
a-reach or rinsed clean taut

please not an om and om smoke
deepens the nonplussed
pulse piling on pulse no pulse

Diptych: Paleo-Balkan Substratum

racing foam

          under scraps.

rubble sun

          pins souls

to razor wire.

          swaddle 'neath

manure; lamb

          breath rhythm

hums, whirls,

          radiates. no

wall, stable

          eyes, stars

after sayings:

          women and

burials. ghost

                "Slobo," Spring

blooms leafless

                trees roar;

acid showers

                birth May ash.

Notes

"materiality" was written using cuttings from the descriptive signs next to paintings/sculptures at the Art Institute of Chicago on March 28, 2006. I included language which caught my eye or ear. Later, I merged the cut language with other lyrical jottings of my own and these sources: Eleni Sikelianos *The Book of Jon*, James Joyce *A Portrait of the Artist as a Young Man*; The King James Bible (Matthew 19:14-15);

"mobilizations": "What's the Matter with Liberals?" by Thomas Frank in New York Review of Books (http://www.nybooks.com/articles/17982); World Socialist Website (http://www.wsws.org/articles/2004/jan2004/2004-j03.shtml)

"Obedients" uses a quote from a newspaper article located on http://www.olafire.com/Home.asp.

"Astrophysical Chicago" draws from the following sources: The Eastland Disaster Historical Society (http://www.eastlanddisaster.org/); *The Sinking of the Eastland: America's Forgotten Tragedy* by Jay R. Bonansinga; "Take You on a Cruise" by Interpol on *Antics*; *The Eclipses* by David Woo; *White Noise* DVD bonus features; The American Association of Electronic Voice Phenomena (http://www.aaevp.com/); Heraclitus; Haunted Chicago (http://www.prairieghosts.com/eastland.html); The Eastland Disaster: A Case of Social Amnesia? (http://www.eastlanddisaster.org/depaulsoc1012000.htm); Louis Zukofsky *Collected Shorter Poems*; "Out of the Cradle Endlessly Rocking" Walt Whitman, *Leaves of Grass*.

"supermarket tabloid tableau" *STAR* Magazine online circa summer 2005; N*Sync "Bye, Bye, Bye"

"sub-ode; aubade; forbid" Maurice Scully, *Livelihood*

"Map of the Hydrogen World" Hydrogen World Council (http://www.hydrogen.co.uk/hwc/hwc.htm)

"Selected Nerudialectics" Pablo Neruda, *Veinte Poemas de Amor y un Cancion de Desperado*; Bruce Nauman, "Second Poem Piece"; "Americans, especially Catholics, approve of torture" & "A victim of torture speaks out on U.S. apathy" by Tom Carney (http://ncronline.org/NCR_Online/archives2/2006a/032406/032406h.htm); Air Force Link: Factsheets(http://www.af.mil/factsheets/factsheet.asp?fsID=122); "Last Balkan Tango" by Richard Byrne, *The Globalist* (http://www.theglobalist.com/DBWeb/StoryId.aspx?StoryId=3904); *The Dada Painters and Poets*, Robert Motherwell, ed.; "Food Idiosyncracies: Beetroot and Asparagus," S.C. Mitchell (http://dmd.aspetjournals.org/cgi/content/full/29/4/539); "Milosevic'sYugoslavia"(http://news.bbc.co.uk/hi/english/static/in_depth/europe/2000/milosevic_yugoslavia/default.stm).

"Gun Variation" merges the concept of Bruce Nauman's "Poem Pieces" and revises lyrics from The Roots' "Guns are Drawn" from *The Tipping Point*.

"Diptych" uses a passage from J. Ronald Oakley's *God's Country: America in the Fifties* found in the critical edition of Arthur Miller's *The Crucible*.

"Diptych: Paleo-Balkan Substratum" uses language from Jean Valentine's poems read at Columbia College, April 19, 2006.

Acknowledgements

Some of these poems were first published in the following journals: *P.F.S. Post, Cordite, Moria, Milk, OCHO #11, The November 3rd Club* and *Alehouse*.

I'd like to thank my wife, parents, grandparents, sister and other family members for their support of my work and life as well as my teachers, mentors and friends in poetry.

Finally, Lorraine Peltz contributed the cover art, an excerpt from her painting "Perfect Pair." Lorraine Peltz is an artist who lives in Chicago and teaches at theSchool of the Art Institute of Chicago. Her work is represented by CherylMcGinnis Gallery, NYC; Micaela Gallery, San Francisco; and Koscielak Gallery, Chicago. More info and images can be viewed on her website: lorrainepeltz.com.

Author

Steve Halle is the author of the chapbook *cessation covers* (Funtime Press, 2007), and he runs the blog-journal *Seven Corners*. His creative and critical work has been published internationally.

Cracked Slab Books was started to provide an outlet for experimental poetry and mixed media works. With the aim of publishing at least two books a year, Cracked Slab Books is dedicated to promoting new American writers and to introducing the English-speaking world to interesting international poetry and mixed media work.

Editor: William Allegrezza
Publisher: Raymond Bianchi

For more information, please visit our web site:
http://www.crackedslabbooks.com

Cracked Slab Books
PO BOX 1070
Oak Park, IL 60302
USA